Winter Flowe

GW01006473

MARK J. WESTON

Flower arrangement by Jane Weston

Photography by Roger Tuff   Artwork by George Gale

Reproduction by Colourcraftsmen Ltd.,
Chelmsford, Essex
Printed in Great Britain by
Tindal Press, Chelmsford, Essex

THE FOUR SEASONS PUBLISHING COMPANY (IRELAND) LTD.
26 Fitzwilliam Square, Dublin 2

Main U.K. Distributors : FOUR SEASONS PUBLICATIONS
The Stables, Monxton, Nr. Andover, Hants, SP11 8AT.

SBN 901131 02 4

PREFACE

If you have but two pennies to spend
spend one penny on bread so as to keep you alive.
Spend the other penny on flowers so as to provide
a reason for living. Chinese proverb.

When the bleak winter descends and all is grey, chill and cheerless, flowers with their warmth and colour really do provide a reason for living. With a few flowers a room can be brightened and warmed out of all recognition.

During the winter when the garden is bare flowers come from either the heated glass-house or from the more sunny climes. Consequently you will tend to get rather less than at other times for the same expenditure.

A few flowers however can be used to create a charming arrangement and this book concentrates upon those types of arrangement which are modest with their flower requirements.

Flowering and foliage plants by themselves or in conjunction with cut-flowers are well worth considering as they represent outstanding value.

All your ingenuity will be tested to produce beautiful flower arrangements from so little. I hope you will consequently find the ideas and basic technique instructions in this book of value and that you will soon find that the world's most popular and satisfying pastime—flower arranging—can still be enjoyed and pursued, even during the dark frugal days of winter.

MARK J. WESTON

CONTENTS

"Oasis"

Pinholders

Chicken Wire & Scissors

EQUIPMENT

"Oasis" is a water absorbent plastic foam which is available from your flower shop in several shapes and sizes. Flower stems inserted into "Oasis" are held firmly in position. It should be well soaked in water before use and can be cut with a table knife to the required size. After the flowers have been arranged it is important to keep the "Oasis" continually moist by adding water. When the flowers are finally spent the "Oasis" can be used for subsequent arrangements. There are other plastic foam mounts available such as "Florapak" "Stemfix" and "Savannah" but "Oasis" has been used for all the arrangements in this book.

Pinholders in many shapes and sizes are available from your flower shop. They are a useful substitute for "Oasis" particularly when line arrangements in shallow dishes are required. They can also be used in conjunction with "Oasis" or wire-netting (see below).

Chicken Wire. 2" chicken wire-netting is also an inexpensive flower arranging medium. It would be cut from the roll and crumpled up before insertion into the container.

Scissors. When arranging flowers it is most desirable to use a pair of special

flower scissors. These have one blade with a serrated edge designed to stop the scissors from slipping on the flower stem. They are readily available from your flower shop.

Compost. When planting bowls it is desirable to use a special potting compost rather than unsatisfactory soil from the garden.

Compost

Sprayer. An atomizer spray is very useful for spraying arrangements with water after completion. The tiny water droplets help to keep the flowers and foliage in fresh condition.

Gold paint. An aerosol of gold paint is the best way to gild beech leaves. Picture shows beech before and after spraying.

Sprayer

Gold paint

CONTAINERS

The choice of flowers for a particular style of arrangement governs the selection of the container. It is important that there should be compatibility in this respect. In this book twelve different containers have been used for the seventeen arrangements involved and they should all be inexpensively available from your flower shop.

Small plastic bowl. An ordinary inexpensive bowl when filled with "Oasis" can be very versatile as far as flower arranging is concerned.

Large plastic bowl. Similar attributes as for its smaller counterpart. Also suitable for planted bowls.

Small plastic bowl   Large plastic bowl

Pottery "Oasis" container. These containers are specially made to take a cylindrical block of "Oasis". An increasingly wide range of different shapes and sizes are becoming available. Very versatile.

Wineglass. Glasses make charming containers for the petite type of arrangement.

Pottery "Oasis" container   Wineglass

Shell   Pedestal vase

Oblong trough   Square trough

Plastic "Oasis" container   Copper jug

Shell. Both natural and china shells provide useful and unusual receptacles for flower arranging.

Pedestal vase. Most suitable for the triangular type of arrangement. The pedestal raises the bowl sufficiently from the table to allow full advantage to be taken of any natural flower or foliage curves.

Oblong trough. Made of rough pottery and inexpensive this container lends itself particularly to Line and L-shaped arrangements when simple flowers are used.

Square trough. In conjunction with "Oasis" this type of container is very adaptable.

Copper jug. An Asymmetrical arrangement enables the curving lip and handle of this jug to be complemented.

Plastic "Oasis" container. An inexpensive plastic dish specially designed to take "Oasis" and provide a suitable container for a wide range of different arrangement styles.

Oblong plastic trough   Hamper

Oblong plastic trough. Owing to its depth this trough is not very suitable for Line arrangements but provides an inexpensive medium for L-shaped and Triangular arrangements.

Hamper. The round lid of this basket sets off a Crescent arrangement to good advantage.

REMOVING A PLANT
FROM ITS POT

1 Holding the pot in the right hand, place the index and middle fingers of the left hand on either side of the base of the plant stem.

2 Turn pot upside-down and gently tap edge of pot against table top to loosen rootball.

3 Remove compact rootball from the pot.

1

2

3

TRIANGULAR ARRANGEMENT

Ingredients
11 stems Rayonante sprays
9 chrysanthemum blooms

12 pieces of eucalyptus populus
(about 1 bunch)

1. 9 pieces of eucalyptus populus foliage form the outline in a plastic bowl.

2. 6 rayonante sprays have been added. The first three substantiate the height. The remaining three the width.

3. 3 rayonante sprays complete the outline and 3 chrysanthemum blooms commence the filling-in.

4. 3 more blooms have been added and continue the filling-in from the edges towards the centre.

5. The final 3 blooms together with 2 rayonante sprays complete the arrangement.

6. 3 pieces of populus foliage have been used to fill up any remaining gaps.

ALL-THE-WAY-ROUND ARRANGEMENT

Ingredients
20 Paperwhite narcissi
(2 bunches)

7 Carole roses
7 Garnet roses

1. Using an 'Oasis' container 8 narcissi form the outline. The 9th establishes the height.

2. 11 more narcissi together with 7 clusters of rose leaves have been incorporated into the central part of the arrangement.

3. 4 Garnet and 3 Carole roses provide colour to the perimeter. 1 more Carole rose is worked into the centre.

4. 3 more Garnet and 3 Carole roses have been distributed towards the centre of the arrangement.

5. 3 rose leaves have been used as gap fillers to complete the arrangement.

Narcissi become available remarkably early and are no longer a flower only to be expected in the Springtime. Soleil d'or, the beautiful golden narcissus, is grown in the Scilly Isles where they have developed early forcing to a fine art. The tendency nowadays, is to cut the flowers in bud so that they last well in arrangements. Early white narcissi such as Paperwhite and Grandiflora come mainly from the South of France. Narcissi have a superb and delicate perfume and are usually very inexpensive. As harbingers of Spring they are a very welcome addition to the winter flower selection.

TRIANGULAR ARRANGEMENT

Ingredients
12 Carole roses   11 freesia (say 2 bunches)

1. Using a small wine glass filled with 'Oasis' 4 Carole roses commence the triangular outline.

2. 3 more roses complete the outline perimeter.

3. 5 more roses commence the filling-in. Note that no. 3 is more open than others and recessed.

4. 6 freesia have been incorporated and fill in the gaps between the roses.

5. 5 more freesia finalise the arrangement.

6. 4 rose leaf clusters fill in any remaining gaps and add the finishing touches.

LINE ARRANGEMENT

Ingredients
12 Sweet Seventeen roses

1. 3 roses have been graduated and established the height of the arrangement.

2. 3 more roses indicate the overall width of the arrangement.

3. A further 3 roses commence the filling-in at the same time working downwards.

4. The final 3 roses complete the main part of the arrangement.

5. 6 rose leaf clusters have been incorporated as gap fillers.

The choice of foliages in winter is mainly confined to either the evergreens such as box, laurel, rhododendron, or to various eucalyptuses and grevillea which are imported from Southern Europe. Pittosporum coming from the milder West Country is also a valuable addition to the range when the weather is kind.

Evergreens last well and are very good value. The eucalyptuses and grevillea also last extremely well and have the advantage of being lighter in colour and texture and provide a variety of shapes. Preserved grasses and rushes as well as glycerined beech are worth considering as flower arranging stand-bys.

CRESCENT ARRANGEMENT

Ingredients
½ bunch grevillea
½ bunch eucalyptus populus

5 stems of single flowered spray chrysanthemum

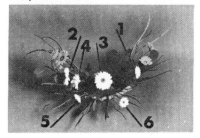

1. Using a pottery shell with 'Oasis' 9 pieces of grevillea and 4 of populus form the crescent shape.

2. A stem of single A.Y.R. chrysanthemum provides two separate clusters of flowers at each end of the crescent.

3. 6 more flower heads have been incorporated (some on the same stem) along the crescent line.

4. 7 more flower heads add further substance to the arrangement.

5. 5 flower heads and two buds finalise the arrangement.

During the winter months when the light intensity in the United Kingdom is low, the cuttings, from which the all-the-year-round chrysanthemums are produced, come from overseas. Large nurseries have been established in Malta, Tenerife and Sardinia, and millions of tiny rooted cuttings are flown into England to regularly supply the specialist glass-house chrysanthemum growers with their raw material.
It is attention to detail such as this which enables long lasting chrysanthemum blooms and sprays to be available, in a vast range of colour and size, every day throughout the year.

L-SHAPED ARRANGEMENT

1. A pottery trough filled with 'Oasis' has had 6 iris incorporated to establish the extremities of the ''L''

2. 5 daffodils further substantiate the extremities.

3. 5 more daffodils have been used to define the ''L'' shape.

4. 6 iris complete the flower ingredient of the arrangement.

5. 10 pieces of Portuguese laurel fill up the gaps and complete the arrangement.

The land in Lincolnshire is very similar to parts of Holland. The water level under the soil is controllable by irrigational dykes and the rich peaty loam provide ideal conditions for bulb production and forcing. In fact the daffodil bulbs produced in Lincolnshire are being exported in quantity to Holland because they are of such very high quality.

The forcing of daffodil bulbs requires the greatest skill, and by special heat treatment this beautiful flower is now available from as early as November. Many growers cut their daffodils in the bud stage so that they will last very well.

TRIANGULAR ARRANGEMENT

Ingredients
12 iris

12 carnations
8 pieces of Portuguese laurel

1. Using a plastic bowl filled with 'Oasis' 4 iris form the three points of the triangle.

2. 3 carnations and 1 iris consolidate the extremities of the triangle.

3. 3 more carnations and 2 iris complete the triangular outline.

4. Another 3 carnations and 2 iris commence the filling-in process working towards the centre.

5. The final 3 carnations and 3 iris complete the flower ingredient of the arrangement.

6. 8 pieces of Portuguese laurel fill up any remaining gaps and, being dark, highlight the flowers.

ASYMMETRICAL ARRANGEMENT

Ingredients
8 anemones   14 freesia

1. In a lustre jug filled with a cylinder of 'Oasis' 2 anemones establish the top and bottom of the arrangement.

2. 2 more anemones together with 2 freesia commence establishing the asymmetrical curves.

3. 7 more freesia nearly complete the curving line.

4. 5 more freesia finally consolidate the ''S'' shaped line of the arrangement.

5. 4 anemones have been used to fill in the main body and give depth to the arrangement.

A great deal of hybridisation of freesia during recent years has resulted in a much extended colour range as well as bigger and more substantial stems and flowers. With their subtle scent (particularly with the new double flowered varieties) and long lasting attributes, the freesia is fast becoming a firm favourite with flower lovers.
As with other flowers the bottom of the stems can become blocked with congealed sap. Consequently $\frac{1}{2}''$ should be removed before arranging, so that water can flow up the stems unimpeded. Fresh flowers are thirsty—keep the container topped up with water.

ALL-THE-WAY-ROUND ARRANGEMENT

Ingredients
12 Rose Copeland tulips
24 anemones

10 small pieces of eucalyptus populus

1. 2 tulips and 4 anemones outline the arrangement using an 'Oasis' container.

2. 2 tulips and 7 anemones complete the oval outline. 1 central tulip has been used to establish the height.

3. 4 tulips and 1 anemone have been incorporated and commence the filling-in process.

4. 3 tulips and 5 anemones continue the build-up to the central point.

5. 7 more anemones complete the flower content of the arrangement.

6. 10 pieces of eucalyptus populus have been used as gap-fillers.

LINE ARRANGEMENT

Ingredients Bun moss
7 iris

1. Using a brown pottery rectangular trough and a pin-holder, 2 iris establish the height of the arrangement.

2. 2 more iris continue the line downwards.

3. 3 iris complete the line of the arrangement. No. 3 projects forwards.

4. 5 pieces of iris foliage have been added to lessen the austerity of the arrangement.

5. Moss has been incorporated to cover the pin-holder and provide the finishing touch.

As a result of research in the U.S.A. Wedgewood (blue) iris are now available, virtually on an all-the-year-round basis. The bulbs have to be specially treated at high and low temperatures so that they think the Spring has arrived prematurely, and flower out of their normal season.

As far as possible it is best to buy irises in backward conditions i.e. just breaking from the bud, so that they will last as long as possible. White and yellow iris are also available in the winter but they have to be imported from overseas, mainly Malta, Israel and South Afrcia.

L-SHAPED ARRANGEMENT

Ingredients
20 daffodils

23 pieces of mimosa
(say 1 bunch)

1. A plastic trough filled with 'Oasis' has been used to take the 6 pieces of mimosa which start the "L".

2. 7 more pieces of mimosa complete the L-shaped outline.

3. 10 more pieces of mimosa fill-in and consolidate the outline.

4. 14 daffodils have been added at random to generally lighten the heavy appearance of the mimosa.

5. A final 6 daffodils have been incorporated to complete the arrangement.

Most flower shops are small establishments run by the working proprietor. The personal touch makes sure that a high standard of service will welcome you.

One of the matters which particularly concerns the conscientious florist is that your flowers should last as well as possible. Consequently an individual care card will probably be incorporated into your wrapped bunch, giving precise instruction on how best to treat the flowers you have bought and some even have a full colour picture of the flower referred to—making them not only useful but really beautiful in their own right.

TRIANGULAR ARRANGEMENT

Ingredients
12 Paul Richter tulips
20 daffodils

17 pieces of eucalyptus populus (say 1 bunch)

1. Using a plastic bowl with 'Oasis' 11 pieces of eucalyptus populus form the triangular outline.

2. 4 tulips and 4 daffodils substantiate the three points of the triangle.

3. 8 more tulips and 4 daffodils commence the filling-in procedure.

4. 12 daffodils have been incorporated and complete the flower content of the arrangement.

5. 6 pieces of populus have been used as gap fillers.

Tulips become available at the end of November in a limited colour range. Owing to the high cost of forcing they tend to be rather expensive to begin with, but, as the season progresses, more varieties come into flower and the price comes rocketing downwards.

It is important to make sure that water goes continuously up the tulip stems. Remove the lower $\frac{1}{2}''$ of the stem with a knife cutting obliquely, roll the tulips in newspaper, and immerse up to their necks in cold water until the stems become stiff. If, after arranging, they become droopy again, repeat the procedure.

ALL-THE-WAY-ROUND ARRANGEMENT

Ingredients
24 Soleil d'or narcissi

20 daffodils
12 pieces of Portuguese laurel

1. Using a square dish with 'Oasis' 10 daffodils commence the outline. 1 sol d'or, incorporated centrally, provides the height.

2. 16 more sol d'or have been added to complete an oval outline and commence the filling-in.

3. 7 sol d'or and 4 daffodils continue the filling-in process.

4. 6 daffodils complete the flower content.

5. 12 pieces of Portuguese laurel fill up any gaps and provide a dark background for the golden flowers.

Of all the gifts that are most likely to please, flowers come out as a certain winner, and more and more people are now saying "Thank you" with flowers—realising how much a conscientious hostess will appreciate this kindly gesture. Not only are flower shops now able to arrange for flowers to be delivered to any address quickly, it is also possible to have an actual flower arrangement sent. Nothing pleases the busy recipient more than to receive the flowers already arranged in a charming container—which can be used afterwards and become a constant reminder of your good wishes.

CRESCENT ARRANGEMENT

Ingredients
22 daffodils
3 pieces of eucalyptus populus
22 pieces of box foliage

1. In a lidded hamper with 'Oasis' 5 daffodils, 3 pieces of populus and 7 pieces of box commence the Crescent.

2. 6 daffodils complete the outline.

3. 5 more daffodils start the filling-in process.

4. 6 more daffodils have now been incorporated and finalise the flower ingredient for the arrangement.

5. 15 pieces of box have been added to cover any 'Oasis' still visible and complete the arrangement.

After making sure that the stems are treated so that water will readily flow upwards, there are two factors which materially affect the longevity of flowers. Temperature is most important. At 40°F most flowers will become virtually dormant and last a long time. In warm rooms, however, flowers go over rapidly, so put arrangements in the coolest, draught free spot— and move them somewhere cooler overnight. Humidity is also important particularly in centrally heated rooms. A saucer of water behind an arrangement together with periodic spraying with a fine atomizer will check the deleterious dehydration factor.

TRIANGULAR ARRANGEMENT

Ingredients
12 pieces of grevillea
7 pieces of preserved beech
5 arum leaves
15 pieces of eucalyptus populus

1. 12 pieces of grevillea have been incorporated into a pedestal vase and provide the triangular outline.

2. 7 pieces of beech give further substance to the outline.

3. 10 pieces of populus and 2 arum leaves have been used to commence the filling-in.

4. 3 more arum leaves complete the filling-in and provide a dominant feature.

5. 5 pieces of populus have been added to the centre to break up the harsh lines of the arum leaves.

There are two distinct methods of preserving flowers and foliages. Method one is by the use of a glycerine/water solution and is suitable for beech, eucalyptus populus and certain other foliages. The foliage has to be cut in just the right condition so that the $\frac{1}{3}$rd glycerine solution can be taken up the stems and penetrate to the edges of all the leaves.

The second method is by drying, using hot air and/or silica gel, to dehydrate quickly the flower being preserved. Delphinium and larkspur are amongst the flowers which can be successfully immortalised in this fashion.

LINE ARRANGEMENT

Ingredients
3 chrysanthemum blooms

11 pieces of gilded preserved beech

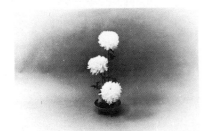

1. 3 chrysanthemum blooms have been inserted into an 'Oasis' container. The lowest one is recessed close to the 'Oasis'.

2. 3 pieces of gilded preserved beech have been incorporated. The beech leaves have been sprayed with gold paint from an aerosol.

3. 4 more pieces of gilded beech help to frame the chrysanthemum blooms.

4. Finally 4 pieces of gilded beech complete a simple and inexpensive arrangement.

Flowering and foliage plants represent outstanding value during the winter and can provide an inexpensive way of providing cheerful colour during the dark months.

Poinsettias are now available in reds, pinks and whites and last well. Being dwarfed, by special treatment, the plants are shapely as well Cyclamon are justifiably popular with their extensive colour range and modest price ticket. Look out for the new 'Silver Sovereign' silver leaved cyclamen—they last very well and are extremely attractive.

Pot chrysanthemums are another 'good buy' together with cinerarias (bright fresh colours), primulas (long lasting), azaleas, solanum (the Christmas cherry), kalanchoe (novel and good in bowls) and last but not least the hyacinth with a good range of colours, attractive scent, long lasting and trouble free at very low cost.

Foliage plants are available in an increased range of varieties in all shapes and sizes. Specimen plants in large pots, although more costly, can provide an interesting focal point—and being mature plants tend to be tougher than baby ones. Most have care labels and it is desirable to follow the instructions carefully.

POT-ET-FLEUR

Ingredients
1 Croton
1 Peperomia magnoliaefolia
1 Maranta
1 Hedera chicago
7 carnations

1. In a plastic bowl, partially filled with potting compost and a small slab of 'Oasis' 1 Croton has been incorporated.

2. 1 Peperomia has now been removed from its pot and planted to the side of the Croton.

3. 1 maranta, pointing slightly forwards to display its unusual markings, has been added to the front of the bowl.

4. 1 Hedera, with its trailing foliage, completes the plant content of the Pot-et-Fleur.

5. 4 graduated carnations have been positioned towards the back of the bowl.

6. A final 3 carnations add further colour to an unusual and long-lasting arrangement.